Lost in the mist

Written by Jill Atkins

Illustrated by Shelagh McNicholas

In the summer Alison went to stay with her gran and grandad in Scotland. A boy called Jamie lived next door to them. One day Alison and Gran were going for a walk in the hills.

'Do you want to come with us?' Alison asked Jamie.

'Yes please,' said Jamie.

Alison, Gran and Jamie set off.
Alison put her hand in her pocket and
took out a whistle. She blew on the
whistle. It made a very loud noise.
'Stop that noise!' said Gran.
So Alison put the whistle back in
her pocket.

Gran got out a map.
'I hope we don't get lost,' she said.
Just then Alison saw a lady in a yellow hat. She stopped to talk to Gran.

'Take the path that follows the cairns,' said the lady. 'Then you can't get lost.'
'Thanks,' said Gran.
'I can see lots of cairns going all the way up the hill,' said Alison.

'I bet I can find more cairns than you,' said Alison to Jamie.

'I bet you can't,' said Jamie.

They ran on up the hill following the path from one cairn to the next.

'Can we stop for a drink?' asked Alison.
'We'll stop when we get to the top,'
said Gran. 'We haven't got far to go.'

At last they got to the top. They all sat down and had a drink. They could see a long way over the hills.

'Come on,' said Gran. 'We must carry on. There are lots of clouds and the mist is coming down.'

Gran began to walk down the hill. Suddenly she fell down on the path. Alison ran over to her.

'What happened?' asked Alison. 'I've hurt my ankle,' said Gran, trying to get up. 'I don't think I can walk on it.'

'I'll go and get help,' said Alison.
'But which way should I go? I can't see the next cairn.'
'We should all stay here,' said Jamie.
'If we try to find our way down in this mist we will get lost.'

They shouted for help but no one came. They shouted and shouted but it was no good. No one could hear them.

Then Alison put her hand in her pocket. 'Look what I've got here,' she said, and she showed them her whistle. She blew the whistle as loudly as she could.

'Someone must hear that loud noise,' said Gran.

Alison blew the whistle again but still no one came.

'Don't give up,' said Jamie, so Alison blew the whistle over and over again. Suddenly Jamie said, 'I think I can hear someone.'

'Over here!' they all shouted.
'I'll come and find you,' someone said.
'Make as much noise as you can.'
So they all shouted as loudly as they could and Alison blew her whistle. Then she saw something yellow coming through the mist.

'It's the lady with the yellow hat,' said Alison.

'We're so pleased to see you,' said Gran. 'I've hurt my ankle and I can't walk.'

'I'll help you,' said the lady. 'I know this hill like the back of my hand.'

And she helped Gran down the hill.

When they got to Gran's house they all thanked the lady.

'How did you find us?' asked Jamie.

'I heard the whistle,' said the lady.

'It makes a very loud noise.'

'Yes it does,' said Alison, and she blew on it again.

'Oh no!' they all said.